THE JOKES FOR 7 YEAR OLDS

FUNNY KIDS JOKES
TO MAKE YOU LAUGH

HOLLI AND ASA WHALING

Text Copyright © 2024 Holli & Asa Whaling.
Illustrations copyright © Sunil Nissanka Amarasinghe.
All rights reserved.
The content contained within this book may not be reproduced,
duplicated or transmitted without direct written permission from
the author or the publisher.

Under no circumstances will any blame or legal responsibility be
held against the publisher, or author, for any damages, reparation,
or monetary loss due to the information contained within this
book, either directly or indirectly.

Legal Notice:

This book is copyright protected. It is only for personal use.
You cannot amend, distribute, sell, use, quote or paraphrase any
part, or the content within this book, without the consent of the
author or publisher.

Disclaimer Notice:

Please note the information contained within this document is for
educational and entertainment purposes only. All effort has been
executed to present accurate, up to date, reliable, complete
information. No warranties of any kind are declared or implied.
Readers acknowledge that the author is not engaged in the
rendering of legal, financial, medical or professional advice.
The content within this book has been derived from various
sources. Please consult a licensed professional before attempting
any techniques outlined in this book.

By reading this document, the reader agrees that under no
circumstances is the author responsible for any losses, direct or
indirect, that are incurred as a result of the use of
the information contained within this document, including,
but not limited to, errors, omissions, or inaccuracies.

Illustrations, cover, format, and layout design by Sunil Nissanka.

∽ DEDICATION ∽

Mike, my partner in laughter and love, and to my two little jokesters, Asa and Evan, who light up our lives with giggles and grins. This book is dedicated to the joy you bring into our home, one joke at a time. May it fill your days with even more laughter and endless smiles.
With all my love,
Mommy Holli

TABLE OF CONTENTS

INTRODUCTION

Hey there, awesome readers!

Get ready to dive into 'The Best Jokes for 7-Year-Olds' – the coolest, funniest, and most giggle-packed book ever!

You know, life can sometimes be pretty tricky, and it's those tough days that make us appreciate the power of laughter even more. It's like a super-secret weapon that can turn any frown upside down! This book is all about sharing the magic of laughter with you, our amazing readers.

We're just like you, and we love making books that spread happiness all around the world. It's the best feeling ever knowing that we're helping you have tons of fun and make your days super special.

'The Best Jokes for 7-Year-Olds' is just one of the incredible books in our series, each packed with hilarious jokes and riddles made just for kids like you. Want to find even more funny stuff? Well, all you have to do is scan the QR code, and you'll discover a world of laughter waiting for you.

So get ready to laugh, chuckle, and snort with delight as you flip through the pages of this book. We hope it brings big, belly-aching laughs to your day!

With big smiles and lots of giggles,
Holli & Asa

Chapter 1:
SCHOOL LIFE Jokes

This chapter has
the 8 best
school life jokes

WHO IS IN CHARGE OF ALL THE SCHOOL SUPPLIES ?

The Ruler

WHERE DO BOOKS HIDE WHEN THEY ARE SCARED?

Under their covers

WHAT DID THE PAPER SAY TO THE PENCIL?

You have a good point

WHY DO CALCULATORS MAKE GREAT FRIENDS?

You can always count on them

WHERE DO PENCILS GO ON VACATION?

Pennsylvania

WHY ISN'T THERE A CLOCK IN THE LIBRARY?

Because it tocks too much

WHY DID THE BOY EAT HIS HOMEWORK?

Because his teacher said it was a piece of cake!

WHY DID THE TEACHER WEAR SUNGLASSES TO SCHOOL?

Because her students were so bright!

CHAPTER 2:
PIRATES AND THE OCEAN JOKES

This chapter has
the 12 funniest jokes about
pirates and the ocean

HOW DOES A PIRATE CUT THE SEA IN HALF?

With a seesaw

WHERE DO PIRATES BUY THEIR HOOKS?

The second hand store

WHO KEEPS THE OCEAN CLEAN?

The mermaid

WHAT LETTER IN THE ALPHABET HAS THE MOST WATER?

The C

WHY DO SHRIMP NEVER SHARE?

They're so shellfish

WHAT IS A PIRATE'S FAVORITE LETTER OF THE ALPHABET?

Arrrrrrrr

WHAT DO YOU GET WHEN YOU THROW A BUNCH OF BOOKS INTO THE OCEAN?

A title wave

WHAT DID THE BEACH SAY TO THE WAVE?

Long tide, no sea

HOW DO ALL THE OCEANS SAY HELLO TO EACH OTHER?

They wave!

HOW CAN YOU TELL THE OCEAN IS FRIENDLY?

It waves

WHAT KIND OF FISH ONLY COMES OUT AT NIGHT?

starfish

WHERE DOES SEAWEED LOOK FOR A NEW JOB?

In the kelp-wanted section

Chapter 3:
NATURE Jokes

This chapter has
18 of the best jokes about
nature

WHAT KIND OF BOW CAN'T BE TIED?

A rainbow

WHAT DO YOU CALL A FLOWER THAT RUNS ON ELECTRICITY?

A power plant

WHAT KIND OF ROOM DOESN'T HAVE DOORS?

A mushroom

WHAT DO YOU CALL A ROBOT FARMER?

A transfarmer

WHAT KIND OF TREE FITS IN YOUR HAND?

A palm tree

WHAT'S BROWN AND STICKY?

A stick

WHAT IS THE SCARIEST PLANT?

Bam-BOO!

WHY WAS THE MUSHROOM INVITED TO EVERY PARTY?

Because he was a fungi

WHY COULDN'T THE FLOWER RIDE ITS BIKE?

It had lost its petals

WHAT DID THE GROUND SAY TO THE EARTHQUAKE?

You crack me up!

WHAT IS A TORNADO'S FAVOURITE GAME TO PLAY?

Twister

WHAT DOES THE SUN DRINK OUT OF?

Sunglasses

WHAT GOES UP WHEN THE RAIN COMES DOWN?

An umbrella

WHAT KIND OF SHORTS DO CLOUDS WEAR?

Thunderwear

WHAT DO YOU CALL AN OLD SNOWMAN?

Water

WHAT FALLS ALL WINTER BUT DOESN'T GET HURT?

Snow

WHAT DO YOU CALL TWO BIRDS IN LOVE?

Tweethearts

WHY SHOULD YOU BE CAREFUL WHEN IT'S RAINING CATS AND DOGS?

You might step in a poodle!

Chapter 4:
SPACE Jokes

This chapter has 4 funny space jokes

WHY DID THE COW GO IN THE SPACESHIP?

It wanted to see the moooooooon!

WHAT DO STARS SAY WHEN THEY APOLOGIZE TO ONE ANOTHER?

"I'm starry!"

HOW DOES NASA ORGANISE A PARTY?

They planet!

WHAT DOES THE ALIEN DO WHEN HE IS BORED AT SCHOOL?

He spaces out

CHAPTER 5:
SPORTS Jokes

This chapter has 4 funny
sports jokes

WHY WAS CINDERELLA KICKED OFF THE BASEBALL TEAM?

Because she kept running away from the ball

WHAT IS A BOXER'S FAVORITE DRINK?

Fruit punch

WHY DID THE GOLFER WEAR TWO PAIRS OF PANTS?

In case he got a hole in one

WHY DID THE POLICEMAN GO TO THE BASEBALL GAME?

He heard someone was trying to steal a base

CHAPTER 6:
DINOSAUR JOKES

This chapter has 6 funny
dinosaur jokes

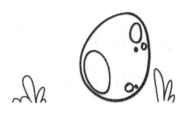

WHAT DO YOU CALL A DINOSAUR WHO WEARS GLASSES?

A Do-you-think-he-saurus

WHAT DO YOU CALL A DINOSAUR FART?

A blast from the past

WHAT DO YOU CALL AN ANXIOUS DINOSAUR?

A Nervous Rex

WHAT DOES A TRICERATOPS SIT ON?

Its tricera-bottom!

WHAT DO YOU CALL A DINOSAUR IN A COWBOY HAT?

A Tyrannosaurus Tex

WHY CAN'T YOU HEAR A PTERODACTYL USE THE BATHROOM?

Because the P is silent

Chapter 7:
Animal Jokes

This chapter has 48 funny animal jokes

WHAT DID THE FROG ORDER TO DRINK?

A Diet Croak

HOW DO YOU GET A SQUIRREL TO LIKE YOU?

Act like a nut

WHAT DO ELEPHANTS WEAR TO GO SWIMMING?

Trunks

WHAT IS A CAT'S FAVORITE COLOR?

Purrrr-ple

WHAT DO YOU CALL A WELL DRESSED LION?

A Dandy-lion

WHERE DO ELEPHANTS PACK THEIR CLOTHES?

In their trunks

WHAT IS A SNAKE'S FAVORITE SCHOOL SUBJECT?

Hissstory

WHAT KIND OF HAIRCUTS DO BEES GET?

Buzzzzcuts!

WHAT IS A COW'S FAVORITE DRINK?

A smmooooothie

WHAT DO YOU CALL A CHICKEN WHO COUNTS HER EGGS

A Mathema-chicken

WHAT DID ONE FIREFLY SAY TO THE OTHER?

Got to glow now!

WHAT DO YOU CALL A BEAR WITH NO TEETH?

A gummy bear!

WHAT'S MORE IMPRESSIVE THAN A TALKING PARROT?

A spelling bee

WHAT DO YOU GET WHEN YOU CROSS A SNAIL WITH A PORCUPINE?

A slowpoke

WHAT DO YOU CALL A PIG THAT KNOWS KARATE?

A pork chop!

WHAT DO YOU GET WHEN YOU CROSS A SNAKE AND A PIE?

A pie-thon!

WHY DIDN'T ANYONE WANT THE PIG ON THEIR BASKETBALL TEAM

Because he always hogs the ball

WHAT DO YOU GET WHEN YOU CROSS A CENTIPEDE AND A PARROT?

A Walkie talkie

WHAT DO YOU CALL A DUCK THAT GETS ALL A's?

A Wise Quacker

WHAT DID THE SPIDER'S BRIDE WEAR?

A webbing dress

WHY SHOULD YOU NEVER TELL A PIG A SECRET?

Because it's bound to squeal

WHAT GOES "TICK, WOOF, TICK WOOF"?

A watchdog

WHY DO BIRDS FLY SOUTH FOR THE WINTER?

Because it's too far to walk

WHAT IS WORSE THAN RAINING CATS AND DOGS?

Hailing taxis

WHY DO HUMMINGBIRDS HUM?

Because they don't know the words

WHY DO BEES HAVE STICKY HAIR?

Because they use honeycombs

WHAT DID THE CHEETAH SAY AFTER FINISHING HIS LUNCH?

That hit the spot

WHERE DO COWS GO WHEN THEY WANT TO WATCH A FILM?

The moo-vies

WHAT DO YOU CALL A SLEEPING BULL?

Bull-dozer

WHY ARE FISH SO INTELLIGENT?

Because they are always in schools

WHAT HAPPENS TO A FROG'S CAR WHEN IT BREAKS DOWN?

It gets toad away

WHAT DID THE WOLF SAY WHEN IT STUBBED ITS TOE?

Owwwwwwww-ch

WHAT DO YOU HEAR WHEN A COW BREAKS THE SOUND BARRIER?

Cow Boom!

CAN A KANGAROO JUMP HIGHER THAN THE EMPIRE STATE BUILDING?

Of course! Buildings can't jump!

WHAT DID THE MAMA COW SAY TO THE BABY COW?

It's pasture bedtime

WHAT IS A PONY'S FAVORITE DRINK?

Lemon-neighed

WHAT DO YOU CALL AN OWL THAT DOES MAGIC TRICKS?

Hoo-dini

WHAT DID THE JUDGE SAY WHEN THE SKUNK WAS ON TRIAL?

Odor in the court

WHERE DO HORSES LIVE?

Neeeeiggh-borhoods

WHY DIDN'T THE KOALA GET THE JOB?

They said she was over-koalafied

WHERE DO YOU TAKE CATS TO LEARN TO SWIM?

The Kitty Pool

WHAT DID THE MOUSE SAY TO THE KEYBOARD?

You're my type

WHAT KIND OF BEES LIVE IN A GRAVEYARD?

Zom-bees

DO BEES FLY IN THE RAIN?

Not without their yellow jackets!

WHAT DO YOU GET WHEN YOU CROSS AN ELEPHANT WITH A FISH?

Swimming trunks

WHY COULDN'T THE PONY SING A LULLABY?

She was a little horse

WHAT HAPPENED WHEN TWO MONKEYS WERE FIGHTING OVER THE BANANA?

The banana split

WHAT DO YOU CALL A LEFT-HANDED DOG?

A south paw!

CHAPTER 8:
FOOD JOKES

This chapter has the 22 funniest food jokes

WHAT'S THE DIFFERENCE BETWEEN ROAST BEEF AND PEA SOUP?

Anyone can roast beef

WHY DID THE COOKIE GO TO THE DOCTOR?

It was feeling crummy

WHY DID THE BANANA GO TO THE DOCTOR?

Because it wasn't peeling well

WHICH FRUIT DO TWINS LOVE?

Pears

HOW DO YOU FIX A BROKEN TOMATO?

With a can of tomato paste

WHAT DID ONE TOMATO SAY TO THE OTHER TOMATO IN THE RUNNING RACE?

Ketchup

WHAT DO YOU CALL A FAKE NOODLE?

An Impasta

WHAT DOES A NOSEY PEPPER DO?

Gets jalapeno business

WHAT DO YOU CALL A BAGEL THAT CAN FLY?

Plain Bagel

HOW DO YOU OPEN A BANANA?

With a mon-key

WHERE DO BURGERS GO TO DANCE?

The meat ball

WHAT DID THE LITTLE CORN SAY TO THE MAMA CORN?

Where is popcorn?

HOW DO YOU FIX A CRACKED PUMPKIN?

With a pumpkin patch

WHAT TWO THINGS CAN YOU NEVER HAVE FOR BREAKFAST?

Lunch and dinner

WHAT HAPPENS WHEN AN EGG LAUGHS?

It cracks up

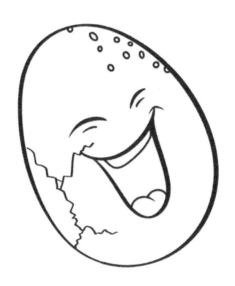

WHAT DO YOU GET WHEN YOU CROSS AN ELEPHANT AND A POTATO?

Mashed Potatoes

WHY DIDN'T THE ORANGE WIN THE RACE?

Because it ran out of juice

WHAT DID THE CAKE SAY TO THE FORK?

You want a piece of me?

WHAT DID ONE PLATE SAY TO THE OTHER PLATE?

Dinner is on me

WHY DID THE LETTUCE WIN THE RACE?

Because it's always a-head

WHY ARE STRAWBERRIES NATURAL MUSICIANS?

They love to jam

WHERE DO YOU LEARN TO MAKE BANANA SPLITS?

Sundae school

CHAPTER 9:
MISCELLANEOUS JOKES

This chapter is a mash-up of all our favorite jokes

WHAT TIME IS IT WHEN THE CLOCK STRIKES 13?

Time to get a new clock

WHAT'S FASTER, COLD OR HOT?

Hot, because you can catch a cold

WHAT DO YOU CALL AN ANGRY CLOCK?

Ticked off

DID YOU HEAR ABOUT THAT NEW MUSIC GROUP, PLASTIC?

They mostly wrap

WHEN IS THE BEST TIME TO MAKE A DENTIST APPOINTMENT?

Tooth-hurty

WHICH HAND IS IT BETTER TO WRITE WITH?

Neither, it's better to write with a pencil!

WHAT KIND OF MUSIC DO BALLOONS HATE?

Pop

HOW DO YOU TALK TO A GIANT?

You use big words

WHAT'S GREEN AND NOT HEAVY?

Light green

WHAT IS BLUE AND NOT VERY LIGHT?

Dark Blue

WHY DID MIKE THROW A CLOCK OUT THE WINDOW?

Because he wanted to see time fly

WHAT DO YOU CALL A HAPPY COWBOY?

A Jolly Rancher

WHY WAS THE BROOM RUNNING LATE?

It over swept

WHAT DID THE COP DAD SAY TO THE TODDLER WHEN HE WOULDN'T TAKE A NAP?

It appears you are resisting a rest

WHAT STAYS IN THE CORNER YET CAN TRAVEL ALL OVER THE WORLD?

A stamp

WHY DID AJ PUT SUGAR ON HIS PILLOW?

Because he wanted to have sweet dreams

WHY DID THE ROBBER JUMP IN THE SHOWER?

He wanted to make a clean getaway

WHY ARE GHOSTS BAD LIARS?

Because you can see right through them

WHAT WORD ENDS WITH E AND ONLY HAS ONE LETTER IN IT?

Envelope

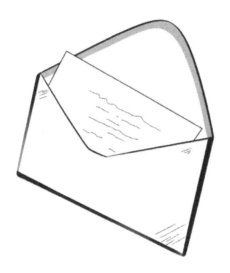

WHICH LETTER OF THE ALPHABET HAS THE MOST WATER?

C

WHY WAS 6 AFRAID OF 7?

Because 7, 8, 9

WHAT DO YOU CALL A SMELLY FAIRY?

Stinkerbell

WHY ARE BALLOONS SO EXPENSIVE?

Inflation

WHAT DID THE PASTRY CHEF DO ON VACATION?

Loafed around

WHY DID THE GIRL RUN AROUND HER BED?

Because she was trying to catch up on her sleep

HOW DOES A TRAIN EAT?

It goes chew chew

WHY DID THE TEDDY BEAR NOT WANT DESSERT?

Because she was stuffed

WHAT DID THE DIGITAL CLOCK SAY TO THE GRANDFATHER CLOCK?

Look grandpa no hands!

WHAT DID ONE PENNY SAY TO THE OTHER PENNY?

We make cents

WHAT DOES A HOUSE WEAR?

A dress

CHAPTER 10:
KNOCK KNOCK JOKES

This chapter has 26 funny
Knock-knock jokes

KNOCK KNOCK!

Who's there?

RADIO.

Radio, who?

RADIO NOT, HERE I COME!

KNOCK KNOCK!

Who's there?

CANOE.

Canoe, who?

CANOE COME OUT AND PLAY?

KNOCK KNOCK!

Who's there?

ICE CREAM.

Ice Cream, who?

ICE CREAM SO YOU CAN HEAR ME!

KNOCK KNOCK!

Who's there?

TANK.

Tank, who?

YOU'RE WELCOME.

KNOCK KNOCK!

Who's there?

WATER.

Water, who?

WATER YOU ASKING SO MANY QUESTIONS FOR? OPEN THE DOOR!

KNOCK KNOCK!

Who's there?

NEEDLE.

Needle, who?

NEEDLE LITTLE HELP OPENING THE DOOR

KNOCK KNOCK!

Who's there?

HONEYDEW.

Honeydew, who?

HONEYDEW YOU WANT TO DANCE?

KNOCK KNOCK!

Who's there?

FIGS.

Figs, who?

FIGS THE DOORBELL!

KNOCK KNOCK!

Who's there?

ICY.

Icy, who?

ICY YOU IN THERE! OPEN UP!

KNOCK KNOCK!

Who's there?

SUE.

Sue, who?

SUE-PRIZE, I'M HERE!

KNOCK KNOCK!

Who's there?

ONION.

Onion, who?

ONION MARK, GET SET, GO!

KNOCK KNOCK!

Who's there?

WEEKEND.

Weekend, who?

WEEKEND DO ANYTHING WE WANT!

KNOCK KNOCK!

Who's there?

LENA.

Lena, who?

LENA LITTLE CLOSER AND I'LL TELL YOU A SECRET.

KNOCK KNOCK!

Who's there?

EVAN.

Evan, who?

EVAN YOU SHOULD KNOW WHO THIS IS!

KNOCK KNOCK!

Who's there?

KANGA.

Kanga, who?

ACTUALLY, IT'S KANGAROO.

KNOCK KNOCK!

Who's there?

NANA.

Nana, who?

NANA YOUR BUSINESS!

KNOCK KNOCK!

Who's there?

BEN.

Ben, Who?

BEN KNOCKING FOR 10 MINUTES. OPEN UP!

KNOCK KNOCK!

Who's there?

CASH.

Cash, who?

THAT'S NUTS!

KNOCK KNOCK!

Who's there?

A BROKEN PENCIL.

A broken pencil who?

OH NEVERMIND, IT'S POINTLESS!

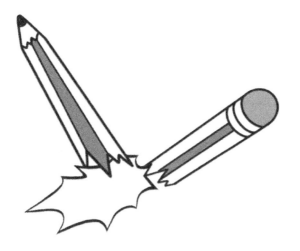

KNOCK KNOCK!

Who's there?

ASA.

Asa, who?

ASA ANYBODY HOME?

KNOCK KNOCK!

Who's there?

OLIVE.

Olive, who?

OLIVE YOU!

KNOCK KNOCK!

Who's there?

JUSTIN.

Justin, who?

JUSTIN TIME FOR DINNER.

KNOCK KNOCK!

Who's there?

OWLS SAY.

Owls say who?

YEP.

KNOCK KNOCK!

Who's there?

WOODEN SHOE.

Wooden shoe, who?

WOODEN SHOE LIKE TO HEAR ANOTHER KNOCK KNOCK JOKE?

KNOCK KNOCK!

Who's there?

MIKEY.

Mikey, who?

MIKEY'S ARE LOST CAN YOU LET ME IN?

KNOCK KNOCK!

Who's there?

WATER.

Water, who?

WATER YOU DOING? JUST OPEN THE DOOR!

CHAPTER 11:
RIDDLES

This chapter has 10 funny riddles

WHAT HAS HUNDREDS OF EARS BUT CANNOT HEAR?

A cornfield

WHAT GETS WETTER THE MORE THAT IT DRIES?

A towel

WHAT DOES EVERYONE ON EARTH GET ON THEIR BIRTHDAY?

A year older

WHAT DO ALEXANDER THE GREAT AND WINNIE THE POOH HAVE IN COMMON?

Their middle name

WHAT HAS A HEAD AND A TAIL, BUT NO BODY?

A coin

WHAT GOES UP BUT NEVER COMES BACK DOWN?

Your age

WHAT YOU DO NEED TO BREAK BEFORE YOU CAN USE IT?

An egg

IT TOOK TEN WORKERS TEN DAYS TO BUILD A BRIDGE. HOW LONG WOULD IT TAKE FIVE WORKERS TO BUILD THE SAME BRIDGE?

None! It's already built!

WHAT IS ORANGE AND SOUNDS LIKE A PARROT?

A carrot

IT BELONGS TO YOU, BUT YOUR FRIENDS USE IT MUCH MORE. WHAT IS IT?

Your name

CHAPTER 12:
ONE LINER JOKES

Here are 6 one-liners to
keep you laughing

What rhymes with orange?
No it doesn't!

Don't spell part backward.
It's a trap.

I got hit in the head with a cola today.
At least it was a soft drink!

Did you hear the rumor about butter?
Nevermind, I shouldn't spread it!

I was going to tell a pizza joke,
but it was too cheesy.

I've just written a song about
tortillas; actually, it's more of a
wrap.

We hope you enjoyed reading
the Best Jokes for 7 Year Olds!

Send us your favorite jokes
to be featured in our next book

bestjokesforkids@gmail.com

Made in United States
Orlando, FL
24 November 2024

54370844R00065